WITHDRAWN

A+ books

DINOSAUR FACT DIG

TRICERATOPS
AND OTHER HORNED DINOSAURS
THE NEED-TO-KNOW FACTS

BY
KATHRYN CLAY

Consultant: Mathew J. Wedel, PhD
Associate Professor
Western University of Health Services

CAPSTONE PRESS
a capstone imprint

26.65

Penw.

2/16

A+ Books are published by Capstone Press,
1710 Roe Crest Drive, North Mankato, Minnesota 56003
www.mycapstone.com

Copyright © 2016 by Capstone Press, a Capstone imprint. All rights reserved. No part of
this publication may be reproduced in whole or in part, or stored in a retrieval system, or
transmitted in any form or by any means, electronic, mechanical, photocopying, recording,
or otherwise, without written permission of publisher.

Library of Congress Cataloging-in-Publication Data
Clay, Kathryn, author.
Triceratops and other horned dinosaurs / by Kathryn Clay.
pages cm. — (A+ books. Dinosaur fact dig)
Audience: Ages 4–8.
Audience: K to grade 3.
Summary: "Full-color images and simple text introduce young readers to different horned
dinosaurs, including their physical characteristics, habitats, and diets"— Provided by publisher.
Includes bibliographical references and index.
ISBN 978-1-4914-9649-7 (library binding)
ISBN 978-1-4914-9656-5 (paperback)
ISBN 978-1-4914-9662-6 (eBook PDF)
1. Triceratops—Juvenile literature. 2. Dinosaurs—Juvenile literature. [1. Ceratopsians.] I. Title.
QE862.O65C54 2016
567.915'8—dc23   2015028920

EDITORIAL CREDITS:

Michelle Hasselius, editor; Kristi Carlson, designer; Wanda Winch, media researcher;
Gene Bentdahl, production specialist

IMAGE CREDITS: All images by Jon Hughes except: MapArt (maps), Shutterstock: Elena
Elisseeva, green gingko leaf, Jiang Hongyan, yellow gingko leaf, Taigi, paper background

Printed in US.
007535CGS16

**NOTE TO PARENTS, TEACHERS,
AND LIBRARIANS:**
This Dinosaur Fact Dig book uses full-color
images and a nonfiction format to introduce
the concept of horned dinosaurs. *Triceratops
and Other Horned Dinosaurs* is designed to
be read aloud to a pre-reader or to be read
independently by an early reader. Images
help listeners and early readers understand
the text and concepts discussed. The book
encourages further learning by including
the following sections: Table of Contents,
Glossary, Read More, Internet Sites, Critical
Thinking Using the Common Core, and
Index. Early readers may need assistance
using these features.

TABLE OF CONTENTS

HUNGRY PREDATORS BEWARE.

Triceratops and other horned dinosaurs may not have had razor-sharp teeth or claws. But many had deadly horns to keep them protected.

These dinosaurs lived between 100 and 65 million years ago, during the Cretaceous Period. Find out more about Triceratops, Centrosaurus, Protoceratops, and many other horned dinosaurs.

ANCHICERATOPS

PRONOUNCED: ANG-ki-SER-uh-tops

NAME MEANING: near horned face

TIME PERIOD LIVED: Late Cretaceous Period, about 72 million years ago

PHYSICAL FEATURES: two long horns on its forehead, one short horn on its nose, narrow frill around its neck

LENGTH: up to 20 feet (6 meters)

WEIGHT: 2.75 tons (2.5 metric tons)

TYPE OF EATER: herbivore

Paleontologist Barnum Brown discovered Anchiceratops in 1912. Brown also discovered Tyrannosaurus rex.

Anchiceratops made its home in North America, near today's Wyoming and Alberta, Canada.

N W E S

■ **where this dinosaur lived**

Males had shorter snouts than females.

ANCHICERATOPS used its sharp beak to cut through tough plants such as conifers and ferns.

ARCHAEOCERATOPS

PRONOUNCED: AR-kee-oh-SAIR-a-tops

NAME MEANING: ancient horned face

TIME PERIOD LIVED: Early Cretaceous Period, about 99 million years ago

PHYSICAL FEATURES: large head with a small frill, no horns

LENGTH: 3 feet (0.9 m)

WEIGHT: 10 pounds (4.5 kilograms)

TYPE OF EATER: herbivore

ARCHAEOCERATOPS was one of the smallest dinosaurs in this group.

ARCHAEOCERATOPS was discovered in 1992.

Archaeoceratops lived in what is now the north central part of China.

where this dinosaur lived

N
W E
S

ARCHAEOCERATOPS could stand on its two back legs to run away from predators.

CENTROSAURUS

PRONOUNCED: SEN-tro-SAWR-us

NAME MEANING: pointed lizard

TIME PERIOD LIVED: Late Cretaceous Period, about 67 million years ago

PHYSICAL FEATURES: large horned dinosaur with hooked spikes on its frill

LENGTH: 20 feet (6 m)

WEIGHT: 3 tons (2.7 metric tons)

TYPE OF EATER: herbivore

Centrosaurus lived in what is now Alberta, Canada.

N
W E
S

■ **where this dinosaur lived**

CENTROSAURUS had rows of sharp teeth to eat plants.

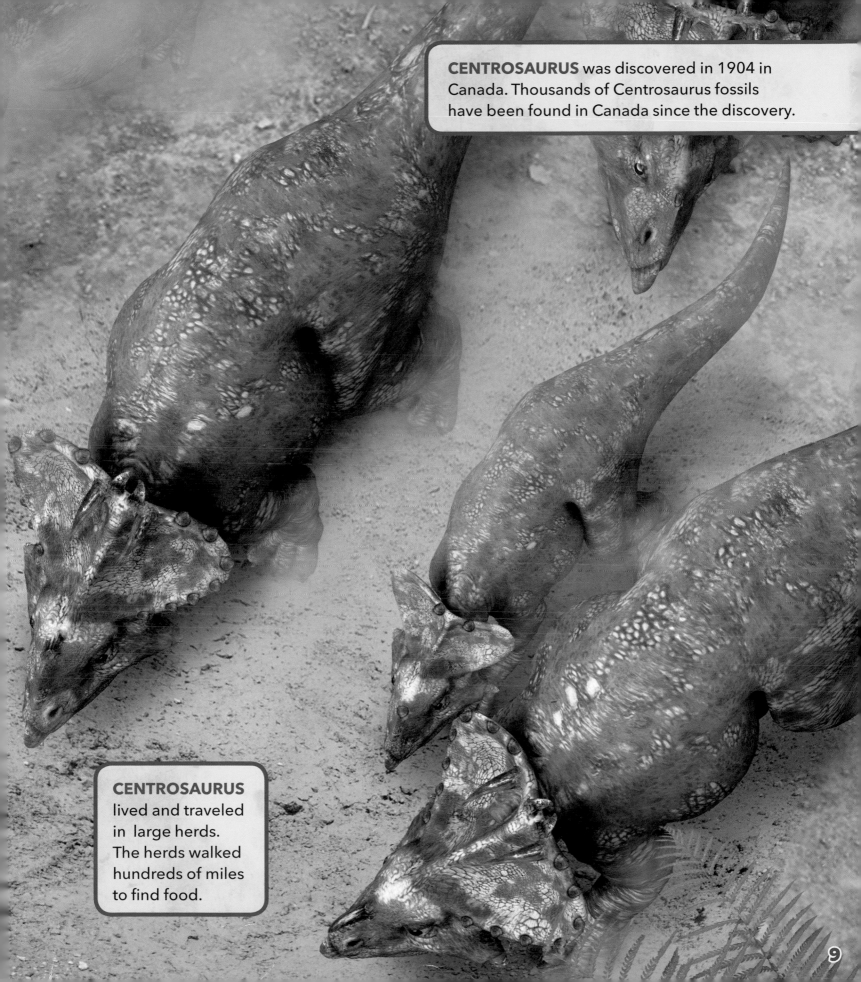

CENTROSAURUS was discovered in 1904 in Canada. Thousands of Centrosaurus fossils have been found in Canada since the discovery.

CENTROSAURUS lived and traveled in large herds. The herds walked hundreds of miles to find food.

GRACILICERATOPS

PRONOUNCED: GRAS-i-li-SAIR-uh-tops

NAME MEANING: graceful horned face

TIME PERIOD LIVED: Late Cretaceous Period, about 84 million years ago

PHYSICAL FEATURES: sharp beak, bony frill, no horns

LENGTH: 2.6 feet (0.8 m)

WEIGHT: 4.4 pounds (2 kg)

TYPE OF EATER: herbivore

GRACILICERATOPS was about the size of a chicken.

GRACILICERATOPS could run on its two back legs to escape predators.

Paleontologists first thought **GRACILICERATOPS** was a Microceratus, another dinosaur that lived in Asia. Paleontologists later discovered it was a different dinosaur.

Graciliceratops lived in the Gobi Desert in Asia.

N
W ← → E
S

■ where this dinosaur lived

LEPTOCERATOPS

PRONOUNCED: LEP-tuh-SER-uh-tops

NAME MEANING: little horned face

TIME PERIOD LIVED: Late Cretaceous Period, about 66 million years ago

PHYSICAL FEATURES: small body, large head

LENGTH: 6.6 feet (2 m)

WEIGHT: 150 to 441 pounds (68 to 200 kg)

TYPE OF EATER: herbivore

LEPTOCERATOPS is in the dinosaur group Leptoceratopsidae. Other dinosaurs in this group include Cerasinops and Prenoceratops.

LEPTOCERATOPS was about the size of a sheep.

Leptoceratops lived in the plains and forests of what is now western North America.

N
W — E
S

■ where this dinosaur lived

LEPTOCERATOPS
lived in the same time and place as Triceratops.

13

MONTANOCERATOPS

PRONOUNCED: mon-TAN-uh-SER-uh-tops

NAME MEANING: Montana horned face

TIME PERIOD LIVED: Late Cretaceous Period, about 70 million years ago

PHYSICAL FEATURES: frill but no horns, narrow tail

LENGTH: 9.8 feet (3 m)

WEIGHT: 440 pounds (200 kg)

TYPE OF EATER: herbivore

The first **MONTANOCERATOPS** fossils were found in 1916.

Unlike other horned dinosaurs, **MONTANOCERATOPS** had claws instead of hooves.

Montanoceratops lived in Montana and Alberta, Canada.

N
W E
S

■ where this dinosaur lived

MONTANOCERATOPS probably traveled in herds.

Paleontologists originally thought **MONTANOCERATOPS** had a nose horn. Now we know this bone was part of the dinosaur's cheek.

NEDOCERATOPS

PRONOUNCED: ned-oh-SER-a-tops

NAME MEANING: insufficient horned face

TIME PERIOD LIVED: Late Cretaceous Period, about 70 million years ago

PHYSICAL FEATURES: bony frill on the back of its head, two large horns

LENGTH: 23 feet (7 m)

WEIGHT: 6.6 tons (6 metric tons)

TYPE OF EATER: herbivore

Only one **NEDOCERATOPS** skull has been found.

Nedoceratops lived in the woodlands of what is now Wyoming.

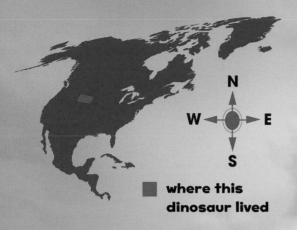

where this dinosaur lived

NEDOCERATOPS was originally named Diceratops. But an insect was named Diceratops first. The dinosaur's name was changed in 2007.

NEDOCERATOPS may be the closest relative to Triceratops. The dinosaurs looked similar, but Nedoceratops had a shorter nose and straighter horns over its eyes.

PACHYRHINOSAURUS

PRONOUNCED: pak-i-RIE-no-SAWR-us

NAME MEANING: thick-nosed lizard

TIME PERIOD LIVED: Late Cretaceous Period, about 70 million years ago

PHYSICAL FEATURES: two big horns on its frill, one big lump of bone on its nose

LENGTH: 26 feet (8 m)

WEIGHT: 4.4 tons (4 metric tons)

TYPE OF EATER: herbivore

PACHYRHINOSAURUS had a huge skull compared to the rest of its body.

The first PACHYRHINOSAURUS fossils were found in 1946.

PACHYRHINOSAURUS rammed into other animals with its bony nose. Males may have pushed each other to show who was the strongest.

Pachyrhinosaurus lived in Western North America, in today's Alaska and Alberta, Canada.

N
W E
S

■ where this dinosaur lived

PROTOCERATOPS

PRONOUNCED: PROH-toh-SER-a-tops

NAME MEANING: first horned face

TIME PERIOD LIVED: Late Cretaceous Period, about 70 million years ago

PHYSICAL FEATURES: no horns, large skull with a tall frill and sharp beak

LENGTH: 6 feet (1.8 m)

WEIGHT: 400 pounds (181 kg)

TYPE OF EATER: herbivore

A **PROTOCERATOPS** nest with 15 eggs inside was discovered in 2011.

Fossils of a **PROTOCERATOPS** and a Velociraptor were discovered attacking each other. Scientists believe both dinosaurs died in the middle of the fight, when a sandstorm blew over them.

Protoceratops lived in the sandy deserts of northern Asia.

N
W E
S

■ where this dinosaur lived

Similar to Leptoceratops, **PROTOCERATOPS** was about the size of a sheep.

STYRACOSAURUS

PRONOUNCED: stie-RAK-o-SAWR-us

NAME MEANING: spiked lizard

TIME PERIOD LIVED: Cretaceous Period, about 75 million years ago

LENGTH: 18 feet (5.5 m)

WEIGHT: 3.3 tons (3 metric tons)

TYPE OF EATER: herbivore

PHYSICAL FEATURES: large horn on its nose, four to six horns around the edge of its frill

STYRACOSAURUS has been featured in many movies and TV shows.

Styracosaurus lived in what is now Alberta, Canada.

N
W E
S

■ where this dinosaur lived

STYRACOSAURUS may have used its large frill to knock down trees.

STYRACOSAURUS' nose horn grew up to 22 inches (56 centimeters) long.

TOROSAURUS

PRONOUNCED: TOR-uh-SAWR-us

NAME MEANING: pierced lizard

TIME PERIOD LIVED: Late Cretaceous Period, about 66 million years ago

PHYSICAL FEATURES: large head, long frill, two horns above its eyes, and one horn on its nose

LENGTH: 30 feet (9 m)

WEIGHT: 4.4 to 6.6 tons (4 to 6 metric tons)

TYPE OF EATER: herbivore

TOROSAURUS was a deadly fighter. Its large size and long horns kept predators away.

TOROSAURUS was one of the last dinosaurs to die out.

Torosaurus lived in western North America. Fossils have been found from Canada to Texas.

N
W E
S

■ where this dinosaur lived

Some paleontologists believe **TOROSAURUS** and Triceratops are the same type of dinosaur. But Torosaurus had a shorter nose horn and a longer, flatter frill.

TRICERATOPS

PRONOUNCED: tri-SAIR-uh-TOPS

NAME MEANING: three-horned face

TIME PERIOD LIVED: Late Cretaceous Period, about 70 million years ago

PHYSICAL FEATURES: three horns on face, large frill

LENGTH: 30 feet (9 m)

WEIGHT: 13.4 tons (12.2 metric tons)

TYPE OF EATER: herbivore

TRICERATOPS probably lived in herds, similar to bison today.

TRICERATOPS fossils were discovered in 1887. Paleontologists first thought the horns belonged to an ancient bison.

Triceratops lived in North America.

where this
dinosaur lived

TRICERATOPS babies had bumps on their faces instead of horns. The bumps grew into horns as the dinosaurs grew older.

TRICERATOPS was one of the largest horned dinosaurs.

TRICERATOPS used its horns and frill to defend itself from predators such as Tyrannosaurus rex.

Some TRICERATOPS skeletons have holes where Tyrannosaurus rex chomped on the bones.

GLOSSARY

BEAK (BEEK)—the hard, pointed part of an animal's mouth

BISON (BYE-son)—buffalo

CONIFER (KON-uh-fur)—a tree with cones and narrow leaves called needles

CRETACEOUS PERIOD (krah-TAY-shus PIHR-ee-uhd)—the third period of the Mesozoic Era; the Cretaceous Period was from 145 to 65 million years ago

FERN (FUHRN)—a plant with feathery leaves and no flowers; ferns usually grow in damp places

FOSSIL (FOSS-uhl)—the remains of an animal or plant from millions of years ago that have turned to rock

FRILL (FRIL)—a bony collar that fans out around an animal's neck

HERBIVORE (HUR-buh-vor)—an animal that eats only plants

HERD (HURD)—a group of the same kind of animals that live and travel together

PALEONTOLOGIST (pale-ee-uhn-TOL-uh-jist)—a scientist who studies fossils

PREDATOR (PRED-uh-tur)—an animal that hunts other animals for food

PRONOUNCE (proh-NOUNSS)—to say a word in a certain way

SANDSTORM (SAND-storm)—a wind storm that blows sand around

SNOUT (SNOUT)—the long front part of an animal's head; the snout includes the nose, mouth, and jaws

SPIKE (SPIKE)—a sharp, pointy object; many dinosaurs used bony spikes to defend themselves

CRITICAL THINKING USING THE COMMON CORE

1. Dinosaurs in this group were herbivores. What is an herbivore? (Craft and Structure)

2. How did small dinosaurs in this group such as Archaeoceratops and Graciliceratops keep away from predators? (Key Ideas and Details)

3. Triceratops lived in herds. Name an animal alive today that lives in a herd. (Key Ideas and Details)

READ MORE

DiSiena, Laura Lyn, and Hannah Eliot. *Dinosaurs Live On!: And Other Fun Facts*. Did You Know? New York: Little Simon, 2015.

Riehecky, Janet. *Triceratops*. Little Paleontologist. North Mankato, Minn.: Capstone Press, 2015.

Silverman, Buffy. *Can You Tell a Triceratops from a Protoceratops?* Dinosaur Look-Alikes. Minneapolis: Lerner Publications Company, 2014.

INTERNET SITES

FactHound offers a safe, fun way to find Internet sites related to this book. All of the sites on FactHound have been researched by our staff.

Here's all you do:

Visit *www.facthound.com*

Type in this code: 9781491496497

 Check out projects, games and lots more at **www.capstonekids.com**

INDEX